"*The Sound Inside* is an emotionally layered two-hander in which the process of writing, reading, and analyzing fiction is an inextricable part of how we come to know and care about both characters . . . A quiet stunner of a play."

— DAVID ROONEY, *HOLLYWOOD REPORTER*

"Exquisitely written . . . Rapp's eloquent language is sometimes meta-theatrical, often poetic, sometimes professorial, pragmatic, intellectual, or wry, and always riveting."

— DEB MILLER, *DC METRO ARTS*

"An exquisitely dark and Dostoevskian little play . . . Rapp is writing about how death usually comes with a sudden awareness of the youth of other people, fellow humans totally unaware of how lucky they are right now, and the rich banquet of possibility that lies ahead."

— CHRIS JONES, *NEW YORK DAILY NEWS*

"A small-scale, unexpectedly gripping new work . . . *The Sound Inside* is a real rarity—a direct, actionless, slim piece that turns out to be uniformly engrossing."

— MATT WINDMAN, *AMNEWYORK*

"Deeply affecting and memorable . . . Rapp's language is a luxurious blend of literary imagery and rhythm and theatrical nuance and intensity."

— JEFFREY BORAK, *BERKSHIRE EAGLE*

"A remarkable psychological mystery . . . *The Sound Inside* includes no obvious crimes, no hint of the supernatural or anything else we associate with bump-in-the-night tales. Rapp instead has written an intensely quiet play of two lonely

T0026123

people circling one another . . . To say we fear the worst is more or less true, but only because we hope for something good and suspect—both from the mood created and the hints dropped—that we'll be as disappointed as we fear they'll be."

—GREG EVANS, *DEADLINE*

"A quietly riveting character study and exquisitely realized piece."

—MICHAEL DALE, *BROADWAY WORLD*

"Rapp is in top form here, creating a tough, dense work that feels more like a recited novella than a traditional drama . . . A delicate play that's always one step ahead of its audience—as any good work of fiction should be."

—DAVID GORDON, *THEATERMANIA*

"*The Sound Inside* transmits experiences of solitude, introversion, depression, and the innate desire for human connection."

—ROSEANN CANE, *BERKSHIRE ON STAGE*

"An engrossing new American play . . . *The Sound Inside* is a potent piece of must-see theater, a magnificent Broadway premiere for Rapp."

—DEB MILLER, *DC METRO ARTS*

"Vital, compassionate and often funny . . . Rapp taps into themes of tragedy and redemption, sacrifice and loss, the bright blaze of artistic creation and the sadness of an unknowable stranger. This intimate drama manages to be both literary and rivetingly theatrical."

—DAVID ROONEY, *HOLLYWOOD REPORTER*

THE SOUND INSIDE

THE SOUND INSIDE

A PLAY

Adam Rapp

THEATRE COMMUNICATIONS GROUP / NEW YORK / 2019

The publication of *The Sound Inside* by Adam Rapp, through TCG's Book Program, is made possible in part by the New York State Council on the Arts with the support of Governor Andrew Cuomo and the New York State Legislature.

TCG books are exclusively distributed to the book trade by Consortium Book Sales and Distribution.

Book design and composition by Lisa Govan
Cover design by Mark Melnick

Fifth Printing, February 2023

THE SOUND INSIDE

The Sound Inside was commissioned by Lincoln Center Theater (André Bishop, Producing Artistic Director; Adam Siegel, Managing Director; Hattie K. Jutagir, Executive Director of Development and Planning). It had its world premiere at Williamstown Theatre Festival (Mandy Greenfield, Artistic Director) in Williamstown, Massachusetts, on June 27, 2018. It was directed by David Cromer. The scenic design was by Alexander Woodward, the costume design was by David Hyman, the lighting design was by Heather Gilbert, original music and sound design were by Daniel Kluger, the projection design was by Aaron Rhyne; the production stage manager was Dane Urban. The cast was:

BELLA	Mary-Louise Parker
CHRISTOPHER	Will Hochman

This production opened on Broadway at Studio 54 on October 17, 2019. The producers were Jeffrey Richards, Lincoln Center Theater, Rebecca Gold, Evamere Entertainment, Eric Falkenstein, Salman Vienn Al-Rashid, Spencer Ross, Filmnation Entertainment/Faliro House, Jane Bergère, Caiola Productions, Mark S. Golub and David S. Golub, Ken Greiner, Gemini Theatrical Investors, Scott H. Mauro, Jayne Baron

Sherman, Jacob Soroken Porter, and Williamstown Theatre Festival. The cast and creative team remained the same,
except the production stage manager was Richard A. Hodge.

CHARACTERS

BELLA

CHRISTOPHER

1

Bella, a middle-aged woman, emerges from the darkness.

BELLA

(To the audience) A middle-aged professor of undergraduate Creative Writing at a prestigious Ivy League university stands before an audience of strangers. She can't quite see them but they're out there. She can feel them—they're as certain as old trees. Gently creaking in the heavy autumn air.

Is this audience friendly, she wonders? Merciful? Are they easily distracted? Or will they hear this woman out?

And what about her?

Ironically, she often dissuades her students from describing a protagonist in too fine of detail. Readers only need a few telling clues:

"The countess possesses a shock of white hair."

"The farmer's mouth is a shriveled ax wound."

The only distinguishing characteristics Salinger gives Holden Caulfield are his height and that little patch of gray hair at the side of his head. If you do your authorial job correctly your reader will *create* the rest of the character.

And in going against her own professorial mandate she describes this woman to said audience of strangers.

Beyond her somewhat forgiving brown eyes, your narrator could be described as unremarkable. In that thorny subjective bureau of classification known as the Looks Department, if she's being brutally honest with herself, she'd say she's perhaps four or five degrees beyond mediocre, also known as "sneakily attractive."

She is the equivalent of a collectible plate mounted to a wall.

*

BELLA

Autumns in New Haven, where the temperature drops so fast it's as if God is hoarding something; as if he's keeping a piece of this world for himself. Yes, my God is a man. He's selfish and smokes a pipe and looks like a perverted eighteenth-century French novelist. My God is a fat man with money who can still get it up. His penis is short and stout and stiff as an old book. My God has gamy breath and gout. My God is basically Honoré de Balzac.

So this is now. Right now. It's the late fall. There has been early snow, nearly a foot of it, in fact. Records have been broken. One barely remembers the leaves changing.

I'm standing in the center of the New Haven Green, a public park near campus. It's very cold. There is no wind. The naked trees look palsied and arthritic. It's that hour of the night when even the most mundane objects seem to possess thought. A guilt-ridden park bench. The serpentine wickedness hiding in a lost scarf.

That lamppost over there knows more about me than most of my students.

I come to this park when I can't sleep. I talk things out. I use long, heavily embroidered, figurative sentences; the kind of sentences I urge my students to avoid. In this park I'm a Creative Writing hypocrite. I imagine my purple prose evaporating in the cold air above me. Thousands of words disappearing . . .

So let's go back in time a bit.

Shortly after the beginning of my tenth tenured year at Yale, sharp stomach pains drove me to the emergency room where I sustained a rupture in my lower intestine. At home I had been sitting in my favorite chair—an overstuffed plaid recliner—rereading James Salter's *Light Years*. It's a book I read every year, often in the fall; that rare work of fiction that continues to reveal new things with each reading. Salter's meditation on infidelity and love and loneliness . . . and divorce . . . and the suburbs and dogs and wine . . . I don't even teach the book because, well, because quite honestly it's so good that it sort of enrages me. Anyway, I was about forty pages into it when

I got up to go to the bathroom and was suddenly doubled over in pain. It felt as if I'd been stabbed in the stomach with a hunting knife. Fortunately my cell phone was within arm's reach and I was able to dial 911. I lost consciousness shortly thereafter. I don't even remember the paramedics.

A few days later, after recovering from emergency surgery, I underwent a series of tests, which revealed that my stomach was riddled with a constellation of tumors. Yes, they were malignant. And yes, according to the medical center oncologist who shall remain nameless, my cancer was somewhat advanced, well into the Stage Two phase of metastasis.

Here's some general information:

My name is Bella Lee Baird. I'm fifty-three years old. I was born at Saint Francis Hospital, in Evanston, Illinois. I am healthy. I eat a low-fat, high-fiber diet. I've never smoked cigarettes. Over the years I've occasionally enjoyed various forms of marijuana but I don't abuse it. Aside from a bottle of red wine now and then, I've never been much of a drinker. I do own a thirty-year-old single-malt scotch. And I do eat meat, but only a few times a month and exclusively the six-ounce filet over at Jack's Bar & Steakhouse on College Street. I've never so much as suffered a broken bone.

I have no children and I've never been married. Like many single, self-possessed women who've managed to find solid footing in the slippery foothills of higher education, I've been accused of being a lesbian. And a witch. And a maker of Bulgarian cheese. And a collector of cat calendars.

Both my parents are dead. My father suffered a fatal heart attack at sixty-two and I'll get to my mother in a minute.

I have no brothers or sisters. I live in faculty housing. I don't own property. I'm essentially a walking social security number with a coveted Ivy League professorship and a handful of moth-bitten sweaters.

Besides those sweaters, my greatest claim to this life has been my book collection, which I've been carefully curating since my early twenties. Everyone from Edith Wharton to Samuel Beckett. I'm a whore for first editions. *An American Tragedy*, *Ethan Frome*, and the French version of Beckett's *Watt*, to name a few.

Scattered among these monuments are three of my own contributions to the world of letters: two slim volumes of short stories published before I was hired by Yale, and an underappreciated novel written in my late thirties that, despite some flattering reviews and a mention or two on a handful of year-end lists, is struggling to stay in print.

So back to my mother.

Lorna Baird died of stomach cancer at the age of fifty-four. She had a rare disease called neurofibromatosis, which the cancer infiltrated. Neurofibromatosis is a condition in which tumors manifest either topically, as moles or skin tags, or internally. In her case, one of the more tenacious little bastards attached itself to one of her adrenal glands and burst apocalyptically, seeding little baby malignant tumors all throughout her abdomen. At the time there was no known protocol for treatment. They tried everything: chemotherapy; radioactive isotopes; transcendental meditation. They even fed her shark cartilage. But the tumors organized their attack and grew so quickly that her abdomen swelled to the size of a cantaloupe.

During the final week of her life I sat beside her bed in the house I grew up in. She was unrecognizable. My mother— Mom—had been reduced to some childlike, larval version of herself. Hairless and wheezing and addicted to morphine. Her hands were monstrous and skeletal. Her breath tinged with a chemical rot.

I read to her from her favorite Anne Tyler book: *The Accidental Tourist*. She was sixty-three pounds. She was blind and didn't know her own name. Eventually, she dissolved into nothingness. Like a patch of snow in a surprising, warm winter rain.

I don't have neurofibromatosis. I just have good old-fashioned cancer.

2

Bella's office. A desk. A few chairs.

BELLA

(To the audience) Reading Fiction for Craft is a requirement for aspiring Creative Writing majors. The purpose of the class is to read classic novels and discuss authorial strategies. And then I conduct writing exercises designed to employ various techniques.

The first novel we always study at the beginning of the fall term is Richard Pevear and Larissa Volokhonsky's translation of *Crime and Punishment*. One of the many things I love about Dostoevsky's masterwork is the way he renders his antihero. Discussions about Raskolnikov never disappoint. I'm always surprised by who connects with him, especially after he commits the two grisly murders. Gender doesn't seem to have anything to do with it. Despite the fact that his two victims are female, the young women in class jump to his defense as aggressively as the young men, sometimes more so. It turns out that Raskolnikov is an equal-opportunity sympathy monger.

One day, while the class was engaged in a lively discussion about the murder of the pawnbroker and her sister, during the only lull in the conversation, a young man named Christopher Dunn said, "Someday I'm going to write a moment like that."

It was the first time he'd contributed to the discussion without being solicited. Blurted from the back row, his statement silenced the class for a solid minute.

It was as if someone had tossed a dinner plate into the center of the room.

"Someday I'm going to write a moment like that."

Just saying it out loud takes courage.

(A young man appears.)

CHRISTOPHER
Can I talk to you, Professor Baird?

BELLA
(To the audience) Christopher Dunn hovers at the threshold of my office. At the beginning of the term one of the first things I tell my students is that office hours are by appointment only.

CHRISTOPHER
If it's a bad time I can come back.

BELLA

Come in.

(Christopher enters.)

(To the audience) He looks around a bit and is drawn to my lone piece of artwork: a framed twenty-by-twenty photo of a woman standing in the middle of a harvested cornfield. She's in all black and tiny in the vast dead field. Spectral. In the distance, there's a water tower with PLANO printed on it.

(To Christopher) That photographer graduated last year and she's currently repped by a gallery in Chelsea.

CHRISTOPHER

Plano, Texas?

BELLA

Illinois.

CHRISTOPHER

Is that you in the photograph? Of course it is. Who else would it—

BELLA

I have no idea who that is . . . Please sit.

(Christopher sits.)

(To the audience) Now he's at the height that I'm used to.

(To Christopher) Do me a favor. Next time you want to stop by without an appointment at least shoot me an email first.

CHRISTOPHER

Yeah, I don't really do that.

BELLA

You don't email?

(To the audience) He smiles. He suddenly looks impossibly young, like an oversized fourteen year old.

I remind him that each incoming freshman is issued an official Yale University email address.

(To Christopher) You should've received one during orientation.

CHRISTOPHER

Email's just not my style.

BELLA

(To the audience) I ask him what he has against it and he tells—

CHRISTOPHER

I prefer penmanship. Getting ink on your fingers. The human effort.

BELLA

How Victorian of you.

(To the audience) He adds something about how one's signature has lost significance in a world obsessed with the selfie.

CHRISTOPHER

Plus, I like the option of drawing the impulsive, inappropriate picture or two in the margins.

BELLA

Oh.

CHRISTOPHER

Nothing too inappropriate. No nudes or anything like that. Just the occasional escaped circus clown playing with a naked toddler or two . . .

(Awkward pause.)

Please don't call campus security. I don't actually have a clown thing. Naked toddlers on the other hand . . .

BELLA

(To the audience) Suddenly remembering this now: one day in class we'd just completed an automatic writing exercise and after a few of the more adventurous students shared their work, we took the customary ten-minute break. While everyone else was updating their Facebook statuses and checking their Instagrams and Snapchats, Christopher Dunn stayed in his seat and looked over his work. It had been years since I'd seen anything like this.

I ask him if he owns a computer and he says that indeed he does.

CHRISTOPHER

MacBook Air, newest generation.

BELLA

So you're not such a luddite, after all.

CHRISTOPHER

I never said I was a luddite.

BELLA

You just don't like email.

CHRISTOPHER

It's more hyperbolic than that. I actually hate it. And don't get me started about Twitter.

BELLA

Yes, Twitter, yes.

CHRISTOPHER

Twitter's for people who are terrified by the idea of solitude.

BELLA

Although from what I hear there's some interesting flash fiction happening on Twitter.

CHRISTOPHER

A hundred and forty fucking characters. Limitation is the mother of innovation? It's more like the mother of mental syphilis! Twitter's basically cheap haiku for the overly caffeinated. I'm not saying I don't drink coffee. I drink coffee. I just don't go to the campus cafés.

It's the baristas who really freak me out. With their Civil War beards and artisanal body odor and those stupid fucking doorknobs in their ears. They're like these New Age, unshowered, tatted-out Hobbits. A life spent perfecting the intricacies of carefully crafted foam art. Gimme a black coffee from Dunkin' Donuts any day of the week, Skippy!

BELLA

(To the audience) I notice that he's dressed a little light for the weather . . . a canvas gas-station-attendant jacket . . . worn thin at the elbows.

(To Christopher) Are you warm enough in that?

CHRISTOPHER

I'm from Vermont, son. Snow is like my sibling.

(Beat.)

BELLA

So what can I do for you, Christopher Dunn?

CHRISTOPHER

I just wanted to let you know how much I like your class.

BELLA

Well, that's nice to hear.

CHRISTOPHER

Yeah, it's a good class.

BELLA

Thank you.

(To the audience) He expresses his fascination with Raskolnikov.

I say, "He's a wonderfully complex character."

(To Christopher) The notion of counterbalancing a carefully plotted murder with good deeds is fascinating stuff.

CHRISTOPHER

I just appreciate how he feels so much.

BELLA

Yes, I suppose that's true. He's most certainly not some callous droid.

(To the audience) And then just like that, Christopher seems somewhere else.

(To Christopher) Christopher.

Christopher.

Christopher Dunn.

CHRISTOPHER

Huh.

BELLA

I thought I'd lost you there for a second.

CHRISTOPHER

I'm here.

BELLA

Are you okay?

CHRISTOPHER

I'm fine.

BELLA

Are you sure?

CHRISTOPHER

I said I'm here.

BELLA

I was going to ask you if you thought Dostoevsky loves his main character.

CHRISTOPHER

I don't think affection has anything to do with it.

BELLA

(To the audience) When asked to expound—

CHRISTOPHER

Dostoevsky didn't create Raskolnikov to elicit our sympathies.

BELLA

Then wh—

CHRISTOPHER

To inspire moral fascination.

BELLA

You like cutting me off.

CHRISTOPHER

It's a bad habit.

BELLA

Well—

CHRISTOPHER

You'd like me to apologize.

BELLA

Knock yourself out.

CHRISTOPHER

Sorry.

(Long pause.)

BELLA

"Leave us alone without books and we shall be lost and in confusion at once."

CHRISTOPHER

Who said that, Dr. Seuss?

BELLA

Dostoevsky.

(To the audience) He studies me. It feels as if he knows how few hours of sleep I've been getting a night.

CHRISTOPHER

(Coy) How old was he when he died?

BELLA

I believe he was upwards of sixty.

CHRISTOPHER

He was actually fifty-nine. He died of a pulmonary hemorrhage, likely exacerbated by emphysema.

BELLA

Did you Google that?

(To the audience) He doesn't answer. He simply sits there.

I expect him to gloat about knowing something I didn't, but that doesn't appear to be the case. I'm starting to get the feeling that he just wants to hang out.

CHRISTOPHER

When Dostoevsky said that thing about being left alone without books do you think he *knew* he was offering the world an
unassailable platitude?

BELLA

I have no id—

CHRISTOPHER

As the words were elegantly leaving his mouth he could probably see them carving themselves into the side of some fabled
oak tree.

BELLA

I'm not sure there *were* oak trees in nineteenth-century Rus-
sia. Maybe a birch.

CHRISTOPHER

The side of Mount Elbrus then . . . These days the novelist has
to either be really good at Twitter or commit suicide.

BELLA

To what end exactly?

CHRISTOPHER

To have his work matter.

BELLA

Wow.

CHRISTOPHER

Wow what.

BELLA

That's not at all cynical.

CHRISTOPHER

Sylvia Plath, John Berryman, Virginia Woolf, David Foster Wallace, Seneca, Hunter S. Thompson, Ernest Hemingway, William Inge, Anne Sexton, Hart Crane, Yukio Mishima, and John Kennedy Toole.

BELLA

But only one of those on that list could have possibly had a Twitter account.

CHRISTOPHER

I highly doubt David Foster Wallace was on Twitter.

BELLA

You might be surprised. Even the purest of our sect isn't completely immune to the digital world. And Inge was primarily a playwright, by the way. I think playwrights actually have it harder.

(Christopher rises.)

You're leaving.

(He stops.)

CHRISTOPHER

The real reason I came here is because I wanted to tell you that I'm writing a novel.

BELLA

Oh. Well, look at you.

CHRISTOPHER

Yeah, the day's starting to sort of slip away, so . . .

BELLA

A novel. That's exciting. And ambitious.

CHRISTOPHER

You mean for someone my age?

BELLA

It's ambitious at any age, but yes, it's particularly ambitious for an Ivy League freshman with a full course load.

CHRISTOPHER

Mary Shelley completed the manuscript for *Frankenstein* before her twentieth birthday.

BELLA

Yes, and by the time she was seventeen she'd already lost a child.

CHRISTOPHER

You presume I haven't yet suffered enough to write a novel.

BELLA

I never said—

CHRISTOPHER

You know nothing about me.

BELLA

(Taking the high road) May I ask what it's about?

CHRISTOPHER

Um . . . I feel like you won't take me seriously unless I go like outfit my head with a crown of biblical-quality thorns or something.

BELLA

How far along are you?

CHRISTOPHER

You really want to know?

BELLA

I do.

CHRISTOPHER

I'll tell you more tomorrow.

BELLA

(To the audience) I remind him that we don't have class until Thursday. It's only Monday.

CHRISTOPHER

During office hours then. Will you be here?

BELLA

From one to four P.M.

(To the audience) I ask him to please set up a proper appointment through the online departmental calendar.

CHRISTOPHER

Can't we just do that now?

BELLA

I really think you should be following the ground rules here.

CHRISTOPHER

All these fucking rules.

BELLA

Whether you like it or not, Christopher, a big part of higher education is learning how to play the game properly.

CHRISTOPHER

Yeah, maybe this game's just not for me.

BELLA

(To the audience) I tell him that a lot of kids would kill to have his spot at Yale.

CHRISTOPHER

FUCKING GESTAPO INTERNET CALENDARS AND DRACONIAN EMAIL ORGIES AND TWITTER-OBSESSED PLUTOCRAT PROFESSORS WHO GET OFF ON BEING ENSLAVED BY THE ENCEPHALITIC PROCEDURAL GARGOYLES FROM THE DEAN'S OFFICE! GO BULLDOGS!

BELLA

You feel better now?

CHRISTOPHER

IT'S ENOUGH TO GIVE YOUR AVERAGE FRESH-MAN WHITE BOY DIGITAL CHLAMYDIA!

BELLA

(To the audience) In my calmest, most assured voice I ask him to please stop shouting. I add that if he'd care to take a gander at my biweekly Yale University pay stub he would see that I'm far from the realm of plutocrats. And then, finally, I suggest

that if he has any more world-hating invective left in the tank he might want to head over to the New Haven Green and unleash it on the trees.

(Christopher spits on her floor.)

And then he does that.

CHRISTOPHER
Isn't that how Raskolnikov would express contempt?

(Christopher stands there, staring at her.)

BELLA
(To the audience) The following day, at three P.M. sharp, Christopher Dunn shows up at my office again.

Without an appointment.

He just waltzes right in.

He sits across from me and without being prompted he tells the story of his novel. It concerns a young man, much like himself: a Yale freshman from Vermont, who, instead of going home for Thanksgiving, takes the Metro-North into New York City.

CHRISTOPHER
At New Haven's Union Station, while waiting for his track announcement, a kid in a puffy coat approaches the student. The kid in the puffy coat's name is Shane and he sports a Boston Red Sox baseball cap with a flattened brim and incessantly chews a coffee straw. He's a white boy from the projects. In

the waiting area he tries to befriend the student. They talk about New York City. Shane can't get enough of all the "NYU bitches" and the "mad modelly lookin' skeezers over in Williamsburg." The student, an aspiring playwright, is planning to go see a revival of Caryl Churchill's *Cloud 9* at the Atlantic Theater. It turns out that Shane's heading into the city, too. He tells the student he's going to meet a girl. He suggests they travel together.

When the conductor comes to collect their tickets it turns out that Shane has lost his wallet. He pads around the pockets of his puffy coat. He checks his seat, the floor, the other nearby seats. No luck. The conductor tells him that he'll have to get off the train at the next stop. The student offers to cover Shane's fare. Shane accepts the offer and the student reaches into his wallet and hands the conductor the money.

That's all I have so far.

(After a long silence:)

BELLA

You spit on my floor yesterday.

CHRISTOPHER

Yeah, that was pretty bad.

BELLA

And you don't have an appointment.

CHRISTOPHER

How 'bout I clean your floor? I'm a terrific mopper, I really am.

BELLA

(To the audience) I call building maintenance and a few minutes later a mop and bucket are delivered to my office.

(A mop and bucket appear. Christopher begins swabbing her floor.)

I sit behind my desk and watch Christopher mop my marble office floor. I take pleasure in his effort. I tell him to make sure to get in the corners and give the mop a good rinse and wring.

He's actually not a bad mopper . . . I tell him I'm intrigued by his story.

(To Christopher) You have yourself a nice amount of dread simmering. Is Shane going to take advantage of the student?

CHRISTOPHER

(Mopping) I'm not ready to answer that just yet.

BELLA

Because you don't want to or because you don't know the answer?

CHRISTOPHER

(Mopping) Because I don't know the answer.

BELLA

(To the audience) I ask him if he's writing it on his MacBook Air.

CHRISTOPHER

(Mopping) I'm using a manual.

BELLA

Oh.

CHRISTOPHER

(Mopping) A mid-century Corona. Recently refurbished.

BELLA

By the way, not knowing what's going to happen is a good thing. If your protagonist is leading you then you'll likely stay ahead of your reader.

CHRISTOPHER

Thank you.

BELLA

You're welcome.

(To the audience) He finishes mopping and asks if he can come talk to me again tomorrow.

CHRISTOPHER

I promise I'll go through the online departmental catbox. I mean calendar.

BELLA

(To the audience) The day after that he returns yet again.

I thank him for following proper procedure.

CHRISTOPHER

Yeah, no one else had signed up so I requested two blocks of time. I hope that's cool. I mean, if you get tired of me just say so and I can go like wander campus and get mentally prepared for the big football game coming up with Harvard this weekend. Stockpile the coldcuts. Get my face painted. Do some steroids. Headbutt random campus bulletin boards, etcetera, etcetera.

(Christopher's gaze travels over to the photograph.)

Has she gotten smaller?

BELLA

I believe she's the same size she was yesterday.

CHRISTOPHER

I keep expecting it to snow.

BELLA

Oh, in the photo—

CHRISTOPHER

Yeah. I have this weird feeling that if I come back tomorrow the field will be covered. With snow. Like twenty inches. But no footprints. The woman's just there. As if the field imagined her.

BELLA

Do you think it would be a better image?

CHRISTOPHER

Maybe not better. But somehow more inevitable.

(Beat. He sits.)

So, the young Yale student and Shane make it to New York City. They detrain at Grand Central and take the subway down to the East Village.

They walk through Washington Square Park and go to Arturo's Pizza on the corner of Thompson and Houston, where they take in the live jazz and share a pepperoni pizza and a pitcher of beer.

The student covers the check.

It soon becomes clear to the student that Shane never had any intention of meeting a girl, or anyone else for that matter.

And after Arturo's, the student invites Shane to stay with him at the St. Marks Hotel.

> BELLA
>
> Oh. Interesting. How many beds are there?

> CHRISTOPHER
>
> Just one.

> BELLA
>
> King?

> CHRISTOPHER
>
> Queen. More like a full, actually. And the room sort of smells like a breakfast burrito. It's awkward.

> BELLA
>
> Is the student a homosexual?

> CHRISTOPHER
>
> He's not a homosexual.

> BELLA
>
> Are you sure?

> CHRISTOPHER
>
> He likes girls. He's never been particularly *good* with them, meaning he's not like some legendary cocksman or anything like that, but he's definitely into the opposite sex and all of their parts and smells.

BELLA

What about Shane?

CHRISTOPHER

I don't know.

BELLA

Good. Keep going.

CHRISTOPHER

Shane accepts his invitation.

BELLA

To stay with him.

CHRISTOPHER

At the St. Marks Hotel, yeah.

At one point, while walking toward the East Village, Shane produces a cell phone, dials a number, and speaks to someone. But the student gets the keen sense that there isn't anyone on the other end; that Shane is performing a one-sided conversation.

BELLA

And then what?

CHRISTOPHER

That's all I have.

BELLA

How are you feeling about the prose?

CHRISTOPHER

I'm not even thinking about it. At this point it feels as if the story is writing *me*. Is that okay?

BELLA

It's more than okay. It's good. It's really really good.

CHRISTOPHER

Good.

BELLA

Would you like to join me for dinner?

(To the audience) I tell him it'll be my treat. He says yes. And after he waits for me to answer a few emails, we walk over to Jack's Bar & Steakhouse on College Street and order a pair of six-ounce filets.

(They transition to a restaurant.)

During dinner Christopher tells me about his mother—a mystery novelist who lives in Burlington, Vermont, in a modest clapboard house filled with books. She rarely goes outside. Christopher thinks she might be agoraphobic. She's an obsessive, meticulous writer, completely devoted to her work. She's published over twenty books and writes under a pseudonym that he won't reveal.

(To Christopher) Sue Grafton.

CHRISTOPHER

She's dead.

BELLA

Agatha Christie.

CHRISTOPHER

She's even more dead.

BELLA

Joyce Carol Oates?

CHRISTOPHER

Yeah, Joyce Carol Oates is my mom. She's going to be here in ten minutes. She's taking me to one of the Muppet movies.

BELLA

(To the audience) Christopher's father is a complete mystery with whom he has no relationship. I ask him where he is and he says something about the hinterlands of northern Wisconsin.

(To Christopher) When was the last time you saw him?

CHRISTOPHER

A long time ago. I might've been like five.

BELLA

Do you ever think about him?

CHRISTOPHER

Do you want me to think about him? Is that what you want?

BELLA

No. I—

CHRISTOPHER

(Mocking the possible litany of questions) What does he look like? How tall is he? Does he have a beard? Is he left-handed? Does

he suffer from kidney stones? Is he good at copper etchings?
Does he have any birthmarks? What's his favorite sports team?
How many pancakes can he eat in a single sitting?

(Bella simply takes this in. Then:)

BELLA

Sorry.

CHRISTOPHER

No, I'm sorry. Ask me something else.

BELLA

I think it's your turn. I'm the one asking all the questions here.

CHRISTOPHER

Okay. Why don't you have any friends?

BELLA

I have friends.

CHRISTOPHER

Every time I see you walking across campus—

BELLA

I have lots of friends—

CHRISTOPHER

. . . you're conspicuously alone.

BELLA

I take it back. I don't like this game.

(Tense pause. Then:)

Am I supposed to be marching in front of Beinecke with some sort of troupe? Is there a "Friends Go Walking" club I'm not aware of?

CHRISTOPHER

Other professors meet people for lunch. They chat with their students while purchasing overpriced health muffins. You're always by yourself.

BELLA

Every other Tuesday I play tennis.

CHRISTOPHER

With who?

BELLA

Whom. She's a visiting professor in the graduate architecture program.

CHRISTOPHER

What's her name?

(Bella sits there for a moment, dumbstruck. She actually can't recall.)

BELLA

. . . I believe it's Lisa.

CHRISTOPHER

Close friend, huh?

BELLA

Names are overrated.

(Another pause. Then:)

What were you like in high school?

CHRISTOPHER

Pretty much exactly the same as I am now.

BELLA

Were you an athlete? You look like you could've been an athlete.

CHRISTOPHER

I made the JV cross-country team as a sophomore, but I didn't run after that. I mostly hung out in the library. Read a bunch of books. Smoked a fair amount of the local weed. As far as sports go, I was basically your classic high school dodgeball target.

BELLA

(To the audience) I ask him if he's made many friends at Yale.

CHRISTOPHER

Not too many.

BELLA

(To the audience) Huh . . . Though there is a freshman girl whom he refuses to name.

(To Christopher) Is she in class?

CHRISTOPHER

No. She's actually an Econ major.

BELLA

(To the audience) He met her in the library. She was reading the new Jonathan Franzen novel.

CHRISTOPHER

I got her attention by making fun of her.

BELLA

How so?

(They transition to Bella's apartment. A rug. A coffee table with a lamp on it. It's cozy.)

CHRISTOPHER

I told her that reading Jonathan Franzen is the equivalent of eating a few servings of truck–stop–quality fruit cocktail and then going on a spirited jog down a well-appointed upper-middle-class street with giant initials on all the garages.

BELLA

Do you really believe that?

CHRISTOPHER

No, but it worked.

BELLA

(To the audience) I ask him to describe her.

CHRISTOPHER

She's pretty.

BELLA

I don't know what that means. Pretty in what way?

CHRISTOPHER

In the same way that horses are pretty.

BELLA

Pretty enough to ride.

CHRISTOPHER

Pretty enough to paint. But nothing too complicated. Maybe a simple watercolor study. Like she's wearing a flattering, autumnal turtleneck and holding a wooden bowl of pinecones or something.

(Bella hands him a coffee mug filled with wine. She has one for herself.)

BELLA

Cheers.

(They clink mugs and drink.)

CHRISTOPHER

(Referring to the art on his mug) Garfield the Cat. "Diet is 'die' with a 't.'"

BELLA

(To the audience) And then Christopher tells me that after he signed up for my class he read my novel.

I ask him where he found it.

He says he ordered it from his local bookstore, in Burlington.

CHRISTOPHER

The Crow Bookshop. Great independent bookstore. Really well-curated fiction section.

BELLA

(To the audience) It probably took a decade to arrive.

CHRISTOPHER

It actually only took a few days. I also snagged your two short-story collections, but I haven't read those yet.

(Bella takes a large gulp of wine.)

I loved your novel, Professor Baird.

BELLA

Bella.

CHRISTOPHER

I loved your novel, Bella.

(Beat.)

It's one of the best things I've ever read.

BELLA

(To the audience) It feels as if a warm stone has been dislodged in my throat.

I tell him that I'm so glad to hear this.

(To Christopher) Published in hardcover in 1997 . . .

CHRISTOPHER

(To the audience) . . . by W. W. Norton and Company, *Billy Baird Runs Through a Wall* by Bella Lee Baird is essentially a social science-fiction novel disguised as young adult literature.

It's about a high school senior, the titular Billy "The Blur" Baird, who convinces his unincorporated town that he's going to run through a brick wall. The novel, written as a diary and authored by one of Billy Baird's less endowed, slow-footed, adoring classmates, Cecil, charts the months leading up to the fateful event. The speed training. The hours in the weight room. The careful meditation. The overheard discussions with a science teacher about particle physics and relativity.

In the end Billy Baird fails to disastrous, tragic, and even comic effect, but his Middle-American town, which has received a windfall of national press leading up to the preposterous wall approach, refuses to acknowledge the tragedy. They *will* themselves to believe that he "disappeared into thin air." Instead of what actually happened, which is that he broke his neck.

And died.

(Christopher reaches into his backpack and produces a dog-eared paperback edition of Bella's novel. He turns to the last page, reads from the book:)

Later I went over to Billy's house to check on his mom. The front door was wide open. Mrs. Baird was kneeling on the kitchen floor, right in front of the refrigerator. Tears were streaming down her face. The only sound was the chorus of neighborhood cicadas blending with the hum of the refrigerator. Beside her were all the contents of the fridge: cold-cuts and ketchup and cottage cheese. Leftover Hamburger Helper and a blueberry pie wrapped in foil. A big bowl of pancake batter and bottles of salad dressing. A half-drunk gallon of milk and all of the shelves and cubbies. It was as if Mrs. Baird was praying to the refrigerator or waiting for a secret knock. The knock would come and then she would stand and open the door, and there he'd be: her only son, Billy Aloysius Baird, exactly as he was before he ran into

Founder's Wall at 22.4 miles per hour. He would be in perfect health, his body glistening and unbroken. But he'd be tired, as if he'd just returned from a long trip and had thousands of stories to tell. Like maybe he actually *did* discover the Fourth Dimension or he floated backwards through some unknown astral body. Or maybe he met God, who really *is* a ten-foot rabbit with silver elk antlers.

Then I would hand him this diary and he'd smile and thank me for being such a good friend; for writing all of this down.

And after that, Billy and his mom would step aside and *I* would walk into the refrigerator. *I* would take his place in the other world.

"Goodbye, Cecil," Mrs. Baird would say. "Don't forget to take your asthma medication."

"Be brave," Billy would add, closing the door behind me.

But none of that actually happened.

What *actually* happened was that Mrs. Baird turned around, took my hands, and I knelt down with her and we cried and cried and cried.

(Reading off the back cover:)

The *Washington Post Book World* named it one of the best books of the year, comparing it to the work of fabulist novelist Robert Coover. *Kirkus* likened it to Shirley Jackson's *The Lottery*.

BELLA

And some of the more absurd stories of Kurt Vonnegut.

CHRISTOPHER

Kurt. Fucking. Vonnegut.

BELLA

The *New York Times Book Review*, however, wasn't so kind. In a heavily qualified review, a peer novelist tepidly praised the overall vision of the book and Bella Lee Baird's undeniably evocative sentences, but ultimately dismissed its two-hundred-and-fifty-six pages as—quote—"a slightly hokey pastiche of dreamy, anecdotal Middle-American folklore"—unquote.

CHRISTOPHER

But fuck the *New York Times*, right?

BELLA

Sure.

CHRISTOPHER

(To the audience) And then I talk about how she successfully traversed the fine line between absurdity and sincerity; how in lesser hands the novel might've come off as antic; how emotionally invested I was in Billy Baird's simple, Herculean goal.

(To Bella) It functions brilliantly as a fable for our capitalistic, celebrity-obsessed society failing its younger generation.

And our hunger for faith and miracles in a godless universe.

I also like that you gave Billy your surname.

BELLA

I've always regretted that. I consider it to be one of the more sophomoric choices I've made in my career; one that begs the reader to somehow interpret Billy as a stand-in for his author.

CHRISTOPHER

Yeah, Billy Baird. Bella Baird. But I enjoyed considering the possible autobiographical tension between the two of you.

Cool author photo, by the way. You sort of look exactly the same.

BELLA

I had a better ass back then.

CHRISTOPHER

Really?

BELLA

I had a hot ass.

(Beat.)

CHRISTOPHER

So where's the new one?

BELLA

The new ass?

CHRISTOPHER

No, the new book. It's been a long time. Like almost twenty years.

BELLA

Sometimes things have to gestate.

CHRISTOPHER

Gestation, sure.

BELLA

And it's been seventeen years, not twenty. Seventeen years is problematic but twenty years would be tragic. I still have three years.

CHRISTOPHER

Sorry.

BELLA

Ask me something else.

(Awkward pause.)

CHRISTOPHER

Why aren't you with anybody?

BELLA

I guess I've always held on to this very simple idea that some-day I would find a partner who I could read with. Someone I could lie beside in bed on Sunday mornings, our limbs inter-twined. We're both lost in a great novel. Something by James Baldwin or Denis Johnson. Lynda Barry. We laugh secretly to ourselves. And we're comfortable enough with our life that we allow this secrecy. Because loving a book is kind of like having an affair, after all.

CHRISTOPHER

That sounds like writing.

BELLA

Okay. At some point I guess I just stopped liking people.

(Christopher rises and exits to the bathroom.)

(To the audience) Christopher gets up to go to the bathroom. As he walks away I find that his youth is, well, jarring. Our age difference is like an enormous cast-iron pot hanging from the ceiling.

I'm suddenly struck by the notion of how one becomes remote in one's own life. Like a forgotten object on a shelf. I am a lamp. I am a letter opener.

A piece of minor archaeology.

How the years suddenly tumble on you.

(Christopher returns from the bathroom.)

CHRISTOPHER

In your Sunday morning romantic-partner fantasy you repeatedly use a neutral pronoun.

BELLA

Are you asking if I'm a lesbian? I'm like thirty-two-percent lesbian. Thirty-two-point-five.

(A brief silence.)

What about you?

CHRISTOPHER

I'm twelve-point-five-percent lesbian. Just kidding. There was this girl in high school. She was in my humanities class. We dated for a bit. Attended a couple of seminal school dances. It was pretty cool for a few months. But she eventually dumped me for a thirty-four-year-old South American masseuse with dreads and a Lexus.

BELLA

That sounds like writing.

CHRISTOPHER

Sorry. Her name was Evelyn. Evelyn Boyer. She played the piano. She had pretty hands.

BELLA

Pretty Hands Evelyn. Did you—

CHRISTOPHER

Yeah, Evelyn popped my cherry. And then we followed that up with a handful of semi-chaste erotic experiences, but I think she got bored. I'm pretty sure every time we tried to have sex we were wearing ultra-festive holiday sweaters.

BELLA

I was actually going to ask you if you loved her.

CHRISTOPHER

We mostly played chess and watched *Mystery Science Theater 3000*.

(Awkward pause.)

I'm about as sexually inclined as your standard, run-of-the-mill parking meter . . .

(Another awkward pause.)

I sort of don't even like being touched, actually.

(A silence. Bella exits and returns with a pillow and a blanket.)

Thank you for dinner and the wine.

BELLA

Thank you for the conversation.

(He reaches up and touches her face.)

(To the audience) And then he does that.

(She brings her hand to his. It's a charged moment.)

But the moment passes—it's as brief as a swallow—and our hands return to their regularly assigned places and I get up and go to my room and close the door.

(She watches him recede into the darkness.)

In the morning he's gone.

The extra blanket is neatly folded on the sofa, with the pillow placed on top.

3

BELLA

(To the audience) Three days go by.

And then a fourth.

Christopher doesn't come see me during office hours.

Throughout the October recess it rains dramatically. For six days straight. A cold, hard, pulverizing rain. The kind that ruins umbrellas and strips the trees of any remaining leaves.

That following week, in class, he seems distant.

After the writing exercise, while he's packing his things, I approach him.

"Hey," I say.

He says, "Hey."

I ask him how he's been.

"Good," he answers. "Busy."

I say, "You've been working hard, I take it."

He says that his novel's sort of taking over his life.

"That's great," I hear myself reply.

I tell him that during class I noticed that his attention was somewhere else.

"You seemed adrift," I say.

He replies, "I just can't stop thinking about it."

"Your novel," I offer.

"Yeah, that," he says.

Just as he turns to leave I tell him that I miss our talks.

He nods.

And then I ask him if I've done something wrong.

"Not at all," he answers.

I say, "Christopher, look at me."

I'm surprised by the volume of my voice, its sudden intensity.

He turns to face me.

His eyes draw out my weakness.

I feel myself lurching toward a desk. I have to brace myself.

"You did nothing," he says.

And then he leaves.

It feels as though I've been struck in the face with a wet rag.

*

BELLA

(To the audience) That night I stop at Anna Liffey's, an Irish pub on Whitney Avenue.

I'm sitting at the bar, having a glass of red wine, when a man to my right starts up a conversation.

His name is Clint and he's a contractor who's been hired to renovate the interior of a hotel on Chapel Street. It's a month-long stint and the construction company is putting him up in town. He's from Bridgeport and has a slight Boston accent, a rust-colored mustache, and sweet, peaty breath, and after two glasses of wine I find him to be handsome and charmingly stoic in a lonesome cowboy kind of way.

I let him take me back to his motel room, at the Econo Lodge on Pond Lily Avenue.

As soon as we enter his room, which smells like some strange combination of cleaning fluids and chewing tobacco, he openly takes a Viagra and we have sex in a classic missionary arrangement with the TV on.

Everybody Loves Raymond.

Just as Clint enters me, Ray Romano's wife enters the kitchen and tells him that she's invited both of her divorced parents and their current significant others to Thanksgiving.

Shortly after the whacky, extended TV family gathers in Ray Romano's living room, Clint begins to deploy a kind of herky-jerky trundling method of intercourse that seems to involve indecipherable grunting, Tourette's-like facial ticks, and the avoidance of acute back pain.

I do get lost in the activity for a few measures. His body is dense and hairy and moves over and into me like some soft rectangular machine that pushes smaller objects toward their inevitable path on an assembly line.

When he's not grunting or trying to avoid back spasms, in curt, explosive syllables he shouts, "*Good pussy! Good pussy!*" Has he renamed me *Pussy*? If so, I can't tell if he's scolding or praising me. And does he mean Good-comma-Pussy? Or Good-pussy-period? Are the *G* and *P* capitalized, like some proper noun representing the Official Legion of Handsome Clint's one-night stands known as *Good Pussy*?

When Clint comes he basically sounds like a woman running from a killer in a horror movie.

During one of the more pleasant thirty-second stretches of our conjoined apocalypse I think of Christopher Dunn.

I dress and our farewell is consummated with a businesslike handshake. We don't exchange numbers. Nothing more is said. I return home as if I've taken a brisk walk and suffered a slightly sprained ankle.

It's the first time I've been with anyone in over two years.

I'm astounded by this fact.

Two years.

A week later I would collapse in my living room while reading James Salter.

While recovering in the hospital I receive a card.

(She removes an envelope from her pocket, opens it, produces a greeting card.)

On the front of the card is a picture of Dostoevsky well into his midlife, thin and balding. His scraggly beard looks like a costume piece. His gaze, which is directed away from the camera, is one of haunted reflection.

(She shows the audience the card, opens it.)

Inside, written with impressive penmanship, in black ink, it reads:

Professor Baird,

I heard you've been going through a difficult time. I hope you're feeling better. You are missed in class.
Your replacement is a graduate student who thinks Dostoevsky was writing Christian propaganda and

that Raskolnikov is a latent homosexual. He clearly loves listening to the sound of his own voice.

I'd rather listen to yours.

Come back soon. I miss our talks, too.

Sincerely,
Christopher Dunn

4

BELLA

(*To the audience*) The consultation with my oncologist yields only the grimmest of prospects. The tumors are rampant.

I ask him what my odds for recovery are. He says they are very low. I ask him for a hard number. He says, "Twenty to twenty-five percent, probably closer to twenty." I tell him that I feel fine. I tell him that I can't smell any rot seeping out of me. I say, "Maybe I'm closer to twenty-five percent." He says, "You're not." I tell him that my bowel movements are regular; that the pain in my abdomen is practically negligible. I tell him how I recently had sex with a man; how everything in that department felt normal. He says, "Good." I say, "Maybe that puts me at twenty-three percent." He says, "It doesn't," and shows me my scans. He points to the healthy tissue, the unhealthy tissue.

I say, "Oh."

"I'm being generous with twenty percent," he says.

He wants to start me on a cycle of aggressive treatment immediately.

The following day, a male nurse leads me to a chemotherapy bay, which boasts a dozen oyster-gray pleather recliners, which are separated by orange shower curtains. There are three vacancies and I'm allowed to choose my very own.

I sit into it. It feels as if I'm accepting some sort of ergonomic, living-room-quality death sentence.

In a soothing voice the nurse asks me if someone is going to come by and pick me up after my treatment.

"No," I say. "I planned on walking home."

The nurse advises that in the future I should have someone come get me, that the medication can cause light-headedness and that the nausea will very likely get worse with each successive visit.

I'm only half hearing him. I'm too busy noticing all the other patients. The catheters attached to the backs of hands and forearms and collarbones and the prophylactic arrangement of the various tubes, ports and fluid bags that appear to be growing *out* of these weakened bodies, not feeding anything corrective *into* them.

Before my shower curtain is pulled for privacy I can see that I'm sitting beside a woman who is so frail and weak I have to resist the absurd impulse to reach over and break her arm. Her eyes are closed. Her mouth is sagging open. She wears state-of-the-art, noise-canceling headphones. She's in agony. I get up and leave.

*

BELLA

(To the audience) Following the November recess I convince the academic dean that I feel well enough to return to class where my students regale me with stories of the substitute professor's bizarre habit of adjusting his testicles while incessantly pacing the room.

I lead a twenty-minute writing exercise whose only rule is that your pencil must never stop moving, even if language breaks down into illegible hieroglyphics. The purpose is to tap into your unconscious and free up the velocity of thought. I ask the class to meditate on the idea of doing something terrible—the worst thing they can imagine: a rape, a murder, setting fire to a family home, whathaveyou—and let the writing spring from this.

I also participate in the exercise, and minutes later I find myself writing the same phrase over and over:

Listen to the sound inside. Listen to the sound inside. Listen to the sound inside. Listen to the sound inside. Listen to the sound inside. Listen to the sound inside. Listen to the sound inside. Listen to the sound inside. Listen to the sound inside. Listen to the sound inside. Listen to the sound inside. Listen to the sound inside.

I fill almost an entire legal pad.

The same five words.

I have no idea what it means.

At the end of class, Christopher Dunn approaches me.

"Hey," he says.

I say, "Hey."

"Welcome back," he offers.

I tell him that it's good to be back.

I say, "How's the novel coming?"

"It's coming," he replies.

I ask if Student X has a name yet.

"He does," he says. "Christopher."

Somehow this comforts me.

I hear myself ask him about the Econ major.

He says that she started dating some senior in The Whiffen-poofs.

"Ouch," I say. "The Whiffenpoofs."

He says, "Dumped for a member of the glee club. Not emas-culating at all."

I tell him he got whiffenpoofed.

Then I ask him if he'd like to have dinner with me that weekend. I tell him that I have an idea. I'm reaching toward something in a dark room. But I'm excited.

"I love that," he says.

*

BELLA

(To the audience) I spend the next two days scouring the internet for the most painless way to commit suicide. There are countless websites. Everything from the discreet, tasteful brightfields.org to the gauche doyourselfin.com, which features instant-of-death photos. There are message boards detailing the process of asphyxiating yourself with a plastic bag and then floating to your death in a warm bath. This was Jerzy Kosinski's method of suicide; purportedly one of the most trauma-free techniques because you lose consciousness before you drown, and the warm, body-temperature water tricks the nervous system into thinking that it's somehow entering a safe, womblike space, so you never go into shock.

Unfortunately, being discovered with a plastic bag over my head in my bathtub seems grotesque and obvious, and, when it comes to a surefire self-dispatching, I can't bring myself to wholeheartedly trusting the plastic bag industry.

There's a Danish "Death Pod" that looks like an intergalactic tanning bed. Like a tanning bed you climb inside of it and lie down . . . but you don't get tan, you die.

Through a few hours of trial-and-error link-clicking that has no doubt infected my laptop with multiple computer viruses, I'm led to a chatroom, where an anonymous, very helpful concierge of sorts walks me through the particulars of lethal injection, which is accomplished by executing a series of three injections.

First, there's the sodium pentobarbital, which leads to unconsciousness in under thirty seconds. The last known thirty seconds of your life, if you really think about it.

Have you ever turned the lights off and counted to thirty?

One . . . Two . . . Three . . . Four . . . Five . . . Six . . . Seven . . .

It's an eternity.

Next is pancuronium bromide, which is a powerful muscle relaxant that causes complete paralysis of the skeletal muscles, including the diaphragm and the rest of the respiratory system. This phase of the three-part process eventually causes death by asphyxiation.

The third and final substance is potassium chloride, which stops the heart, thus causing death, yet again, by cardiac arrest.

Therein lies our brief chemistry lesson.

Three needles. A terminal hat trick. The proper sequence is essential to pulling this off. If done correctly, success is guaranteed.

A sound plan. No mess. No misery. But the trick is that it's impossible to carry out parts two and three of a three-part injection process if part one is going to render you unconscious.

My concierge can't stress enough the importance of recruiting a trusted injection buddy, someone who will see the process through to its conclusion. He or she wants me to type that I am in complete understanding of this.

In all caps I type I COMPLETELY UNDERSTAND.

Through a simple PayPal transaction I spend nearly a thousand dollars.

Vials of all three substances in liquid form as well as three Percocet would arrive at my home via FedEx the following evening.

The Percocet is intended to make things a little easier, advised to be ingested thirty minutes before the first injection.

It is truly amazing what one can accomplish on the internet.

5

Lights up on a kitchen table, two chairs, Chinese food.

Bella is seated.

Christopher enters, wearing his gas-station-attendant jacket, and a backpack on his shoulder.

CHRISTOPHER

Hey.

BELLA

(To Christopher) I ordered food.

CHRISTOPHER

How are you feeling?

BELLA

Good. Tired.

(To the audience) I tell him it's nice to see him and he removes his backpack and sits across from me. He looks wide awake, freshly showered. His hair is still damp.

(To Christopher) Eat. Please. Help yourself.

(From his backpack Christopher removes a stationery box, sets it on the table.)

Is that your book?

(He nods.)

You finished it.

CHRISTOPHER

I don't think it has the heft of a novel.

BELLA

How long is it?

CHRISTOPHER

Just over a hundred pages.

BELLA

A novella then.

(Christopher pushes the stationery box across the table.)

(Reading the title page) To Lie Facedown in a Field Full of Snow. Good title.

CHRISTOPHER

Will you read it?

BELLA

(At an impasse) Christopher, I invited you over here tonight because . . .

CHRISTOPHER

Because you were reaching toward something in a dark room.

BELLA

I'd like you to help me die.

(To the audience) I explain to him the severity of my cancer and my disinterest in going through chemo and destroying whatever quality of life I might have left.

I tell him about my experience with my mother.

I then explain the three-part injection process, how it's impossible to complete without the help of an injection buddy.

I tell him that we have everything we need, how all the materials are in the refrigerator.

(To Christopher) I'd like to do this tonight . . . I realize this is a lot . . . I don't have the perfect thing to say . . . I want to do this.

(A silence.)

CHRISTOPHER

I mean, you barely know me.

BELLA

I think I do, though.

CHRISTOPHER

You don't even know my middle name. Or what my favorite book is. Or if I have like any phobias.

BELLA

What's your middle name?

CHRISTOPHER

. . . Corbit.

BELLA

Christopher Corbit Dunn. That's a good name.

CHRISTOPHER

I have an Uncle Corbit.

BELLA

Your mother's brother?

CHRISTOPHER

Father's. He lives in Elmira, New York.

BELLA

Do you have a relationship with him?

CHRISTOPHER

No. When I was ten I went to go stay with him for a weekend and I walked in on him having sex with a taxidermy pheasant.

BELLA

Okay.

CHRISTOPHER

Yeah, he's a hunter, so . . .

(Beat.)

BELLA

What's your favorite book?

CHRISTOPHER

Old Yeller. And *Franny and Zooey.* And Faulkner's *The Wild Palms.*

BELLA

That's three books.

CHRISTOPHER

They're interchangeably superlative.

BELLA

Fair enough.

CHRISTOPHER

Old Yeller probably has a slight edge over the other two. When Travis has to shoot Old Yeller it's more heartbreaking than fucking *Bambi.* I'm even cool with the puppy being born at the end—it's that good. And Carl Burger's illustrations are individual masterpieces that should be hung in museums . . . And the last paragraph . . . "When finally I couldn't laugh and cry another bit, I rode on up to the lot and turned my horse in. Tomorrow, I thought, I'll take Arliss and that pup out for a squirrel hunt. The pup was still mighty little. But the way I figured it, if he was big enough to act like Old Yeller, he was big enough to start learning to earn his keep." People talk about the end of *Moby-Dick,* but *Old Yeller* . . .

BELLA

And do you have any phobias?

CHRISTOPHER

I'm terrified that if I'm left alone in a room with a baby I might throw it out the window.

BELLA

Oh.

CHRISTOPHER

Yeah.

BELLA

What if there's no window?

CHRISTOPHER

Then I'm fine.

(Beat.)

BELLA

I have a strong sense that you can handle this. Do you not agree?

(Silence.)

I'm with you on *The Wild Palms*, by the way. It's Faulkner's most underrated novel.

(A pause. Then:)

CHRISTOPHER

. . . Okay.

BELLA

Okay what.

CHRISTOPHER

I'll help you.

BELLA

Thank you.

CHRISTOPHER

But first you have to read my manuscript.

BELLA

Did you type this with carbon paper?

CHRISTOPHER

That's the only copy.

BELLA

Please forgive me if I start to fade or get loopy. I've taken a Percocet.

CHRISTOPHER

And I want your honest response. None of that bullshit, forced professorial flattery.

BELLA

(Indignant) I don't do that.

CHRISTOPHER

You do, though. You do it to the weaker writers in class. You pity them and tell them they're good when they should actually change majors. If I hear that guy with the Clark Kent glasses use the word "stelliform" again I'm going to throw an egg at him.

BELLA

What's wrong with *stelliform*? *Stelliform's* a good word.

CHRISTOPHER

It's totally ripped off from *Infinite Jest*. It's David Foster Wallace's word. No one should touch it.

BELLA

Why isn't that book in your big three?

CHRISTOPHER

Infinite Jest isn't a book, it's a fucking planet.

(Beat.)

So, give me your word about not bullshitting me.

BELLA

You have my word.

CHRISTOPHER

(To the audience) It's written in first-person present tense, in the Yale student's voice.

After their meal at Arturo's, on their way to the St. Marks Hotel, Shane and Christopher stop at a nearby gift shop, where Christopher purchases a large Statue of Liberty paperweight, a souvenir for his mother, who he plans on going to visit after attending the play at the Atlantic Theater.

BELLA

(To the audience) Like his author, Narrator Christopher is from Vermont and his mother, who he tells Shane is agoraphobic, lives in a modest house in Burlington.

CHRISTOPHER

(To the audience) As Christopher and Shane get settled into their fourth-floor hotel room, whose lone window overlooks the Bowery, there is a long section of dialogue during which Shane reveals that he is the father of an infant son, whom he refers to as his *Little Golden State Warrior*.

While Christopher unpacks his few belongings and sets his toiletries on a small shelf in the bathroom, it starts to rain.

BELLA

From the bathroom I can hear the rain pelting our hotel room window. It sounds like soft gravel being thrown at a hated neighborhood house.

CHRISTOPHER

(To the audience) Shane confesses that he's been having a hard time with Kimmy, his girlfriend and the mother of his child, who is back in New Haven, where they live in the basement of Kimmy's mother's house.

"So you weren't actually planning on meeting a girl," Christopher says from the bathroom.

"Nah," Shane admits from the bed. "I just needed to get my ass out the house for a minute."

Later, Shane is in the bathroom and Christopher is on the bed. While Shane is washing his face and reciting some Vince Staples lyrics, Christopher approaches the bathroom, clutching the Statue of Liberty paperweight. And he strikes Shane over the back of the head, and continues striking him until his brains spill out through two competing orifices.

After Christopher cleans the mess in the bathroom, he arranges Shane on the bed and places two folded towels under the wounds in the back of his head. He frisks the pockets of Shane's puffy coat and finds his iPhone, the earbuds, and, most surprisingly, a knot of several twenties secured with a rubberband. He dons Shane's Boston Red Sox cap, gathers his things, leaves the hotel, hails a cab, and heads across town to Penn Station, where he takes Amtrak north to Burlington, Vermont, foregoing the play at the Atlantic Theater.

On the train he discovers that Shane's iPhone doesn't require a security code and he scrolls through all of Shane's contacts and looks at photos of his son and girlfriend and listens to a playlist of Shane's favorite rap songs.

Back home in Burlington he has Thanksgiving dinner with his mother and tells her about his early weeks at Yale, where he is especially enjoying a Creative Writing class.

He also likes his Statistics seminar and he may have a crush on a girl who he keeps running into at the library. His mother is so glad he's decided to come home—she's terribly lonely as it turns out—and before he leaves he gives her the Statue of Liberty paperweight, which he was sure to thoroughly scrub with soap and water. His mother is so moved by the gift she cries, and cries, and cries. She's never been to New York City, after all. She's only dreamed of it.

When Christopher returns to New Haven he doesn't attend his classes, but, rather, tracks down Shane's girlfriend, Kimmy, who works at the local grocery store as a checkout clerk. He approaches her register with a quart of milk and introduces himself and asks her to coffee. He finds the brown-eyed brunette with the tired smile to be hauntingly attractive.

Kimmy agrees to meet him and over coffee they quickly connect and she tells Christopher about her missing boyfriend, Shane, whom she believes ran away.

BELLA

"I know he ain't never comin' back,"

CHRISTOPHER

She tells Christopher when he walks her home.

BELLA

"that boy never had no business bein' a father."

CHRISTOPHER

Before they say good night they exchange phone numbers.

Christopher and Kimmy see each other several more times, and within a month, Christopher has moved his few belongings out of campus housing and into the basement of Kimmy's mother's house, where he helps them raise Shane's infant son—

BELLA

Whose name happens to be Billy.

CHRISTOPHER

A week later, they leave Billy with Kimmy's mother while they attend a show at a Yale University student art gallery—

BELLA

Where Christopher is drawn to a twenty-by-twenty painting of a man lying facedown in a snowy field. The figure in the painting is described as wearing a jacket that's quote—"too thin for the weather"—unquote.

CHRISTOPHER

Shane's disappearance never resurfaces and at the apparent height of Christopher's state of well-being and domestic bliss, in the middle of a snowy night, he walks out of Kimmy's mother's house.

BELLA

"Where you goin'?"

CHRISTOPHER

Kimmy asks as he's almost through the door.

"I just need some air."

BELLA

"You'll freeze to death in that."

CHRISTOPHER

"I'll be okay."

BELLA

He kisses her on the forehead and walks away.

The story ends with an ellipsis . . .

(After a beat:)

CHRISTOPHER

(To Bella) Go on. Let me have it.

BELLA

It's very powerful, Christopher.

CHRISTOPHER

The ending isn't right.

BELLA

It works.

CHRISTOPHER

But do you think it's an actual ending?

BELLA

Why wouldn't it be?

CHRISTOPHER

I worry that it doesn't feel inevitable. You always talk about that in class.

BELLA

He walks out into the night. I think it's wonderfully interpretable.

CHRISTOPHER

Do you think he's coming back?

BELLA

No.

(To the audience) I tell him that his sentences are stunning, that his dialogue is sharp and essential.

(To Christopher) Sometimes you mix your metaphors, but even that feels honest because your narrator is a freshman who's also probably prone to mixing his metaphors.

CHRISTOPHER

That's not intentional.

BELLA

Well it works.

CHRISTOPHER

It's clumsy.

BELLA

There's nothing clumsy about it. It's tragic and mysterious and your prose is beautifully restrained. You manage to make me root for a murderer and I can't explain why. His hard actions completely define him. He gives his mother the fucking murder weapon, and yet you never editorialize or beg my sympathy in any way.

CHRISTOPHER

You're also pretty high.

BELLA

Just accept the fucking praise, Christopher.

CHRISTOPHER

I accept.

BELLA

(*To the audience*) The next phase of the evening is cloudy, dreamlike.

I remember carefully placing Christopher's manuscript back in its stationery box.

I remember opening my refrigerator and removing the three clearly marked hypos from the butter cubby and giving Christopher a quick tutorial on their sequence . . . I remember him repeating this sequence back to me with a detached, clinical authority.

I remember asking him to help me to my bedroom because I'm now high on Percocet.

I remember Christopher helping me lay down on my bed.

I remember having cottonmouth and feeling like my face is plagued by a wolfish, permanent grin.

I remember that lying down takes forever and telling Christopher that I want him to have my first edition of James Salter's *Light Years*.

My mind is overcome with memories . . .

The lake I swam in as a girl . . .

Our family's summer home in Michigan, its gutters choked with leaves . . .

As he is about to inject the sodium pentobarbital, Christopher asks me if I'm absolutely sure that I want to do this.

"I'm absolutely sure," I say.

He gives me the first injection. I feel the slightest burn pass through the back of my hand and enter my vein. I start to count to thirty. One . . . Two . . . Three . . . Each number is a building I must scale with my bare hands. Four . . . Five . . . Six . . .

I remember Chicago's Shedd Aquarium . . . second-grade field trip . . . the brilliant moon jelly pulsating in its tank . . . but I want to see the giant female octopus . . . she will live longer than any other octopus . . . She will mate only once . . . Seven . . . Eight . . . Nine . . . *Oh, there she is* . . .

EPILOGUE

BELLA

(To the audience) When I wake up, some seventeen hours later, Christopher's gone.

The second and third hypos are resting on the chair where he was sitting beside my bed, their syringes still full, untouched.

I shuffle out to the kitchen and see that the stationery box containing Christopher's novella is still on the table.

I remove the lid. I read the cover page, which I only half noticed the first time:

To Lie Facedown in a Field Full of Snow.

Nothing else.

A work of fiction attributed to no one and without a copyright line.

Oh, and a short epigraph on the other side of the title page:

> We sometimes encounter people, even perfect strangers, who begin to interest us at first sight, somehow suddenly, all at once, before a word is spoken.
> —Fyodor Dostoevsky

*

BELLA

(*To the audience*) Christopher doesn't show up in class that week. His body was found by a fellow student, on the New Haven Green, in the middle of the night. He was lying facedown in the snow. The cause of death, hypothermia. He was wearing his gas-station-attendant jacket. No hat, no scarf, no gloves.

His death is hardly known around campus. It's barely a footnote, scarcely legible.

It turns out that he'd been attending his other classes more and more infrequently as the fall term came to its end; one class not at all.

His other professors barely knew him.

In late December, while campus is quiet, Christopher's mother comes to identify the body and take it back to Burlington, where he would be buried in some minor cemetery near Lake Champlain.

It's strange considering a winter burial during the holiday season. A pair of anonymous men shoveling through a hide of heavy snow only to break the earth and shovel more.

Christopher Corbit Dunn, interred in the cold earth.

In January, I begin chemotherapy treatments.

I take the spring term off and watch my hair fall out in clumps.

Six months later, at my bimonthly checkup, my oncologist informs me that the tumors in my stomach have all but disappeared. My cancer has gone into remission. He says he's never seen anything like it. He sounds disappointed.

I walk home. Over three miles. I walk past houses and lampposts and trees and office buildings with big glass windows.

It feels as if I'm made of yarn.

I spend the next week eating like a horse. Oysters and sardines and cold ravioli right out of the can.

I devour a whole chicken and lick the bones dry.

I feel as if I will live forever.

For the better part of a month I read and reread Christopher Dunn's novella. I carry it around from room to room in its stationery box like some perfect woodland creature that should never be touched. I sleep beside it. I wake with it. When I take a bath I place it on the top of the toilet tank.

He failed to number page seventy-eight. It goes seventy-seven, then nothing, then seventy-nine. He was so caught up in the writing that he forgot to enumerate a page.

It's one of the most honest things I've ever read.

I'm still struck by the ending. Christopher leaves his reader with an ellipsis; three successive periods, composed on a manual typewriter, their depressions rendered with an almost gentle violence, each one as perfect as a moon.

Did he slip and fall?

Did he collapse from exhaustion?

Did some vital pinion inside him snap in half from frustration or jealousy or endless yearning?

Or was it a matter of the heart even more treacherous than that: loneliness.

Was he drunk with the night sky? Spellbound by the infinitesimal swaying of these ancient trees?

Or did he stage his own death?

Were there footprints?

Did this park *imagine* his body?

Would that be a better image?

(*The lights fade on Bella.*)

END OF PLAY

ADAM RAPP is an award-winning playwright, director, novelist, and filmmaker. He is the author of numerous plays, including *Nocturne* (American Repertory Theater, New York Theatre Workshop), *Finer Noble Gases* (26th Humana Festival; Edinburgh Fringe, Fringe First Award), *Stone Cold Dead Serious* (A.R.T., Edge Theatre), *Blackbird* (Bush Theatre, Edge Theatre), *Essential Self-Defense* (Playwrights Horizons/Edge Theatre), *The Metal Children* (Vineyard Theatre), *The Hallway Trilogy* (Rattlestick), *Dreams of Flying Dreams of Falling* (Atlantic Theater Company), *The Purple Lights of Joppa Illinois* (Southcoast Repertory, Atlantic Theater Company), and *Red Light Winter* (Steppenwolf, Barrow Street Theatre; Chicago's Jeff Award for Best New Work, Obie Award, Pulitzer Prize finalist).

His playwriting honors include Boston's Elliot Norton Award, the Helen Merrill Award, the 2006 Princess Grace Statue, a Lucille Lortel Playwright's Fellowship, the Benjamin H. Danks Award from the American Academy of Arts and Letters, and the PEN/Laura Pels International Foundation for Theater Award.

He is also the author of the novels *Know Your Beholder*, *The Year of Endless Sorrows*, and nine works of fiction for young adults, including *Under the Wolf, Under The Dog* (finalist *Los Angeles Times* Book Prize); *Punkzilla* (Michael L. Printz Honor Book); and *33 Snowfish* (*Booklist*'s 50 Best YA Books of All Time).

He also wrote and directed the feature films *Winter Passing* (Official Selection of the 2005 Toronto Film Festival) and *Blackbird* (2006 Edinburgh International Film Festival, Best Narrative Feature at the Charlotte Film Festival, Special Achievement in Directing Award from the Florida International Film Festival).

He lives in New York City and Woodstock, New York.